Table of Contents

Bad

Just how bad is bad? What one person calls "bad" another might call "good," or vice versa. But **plundering**, **sabotaging**, and committing mass murder just for power? Everyone can agree that's bad. And that's what the bad guys and gals of ancient times have in common. They wanted power and nothing was going to get in their way.

What's Bad?

The dictionary defines *bad* as "evil, wicked, and rotten." Does that describe all the folks in this book? Read on and decide.

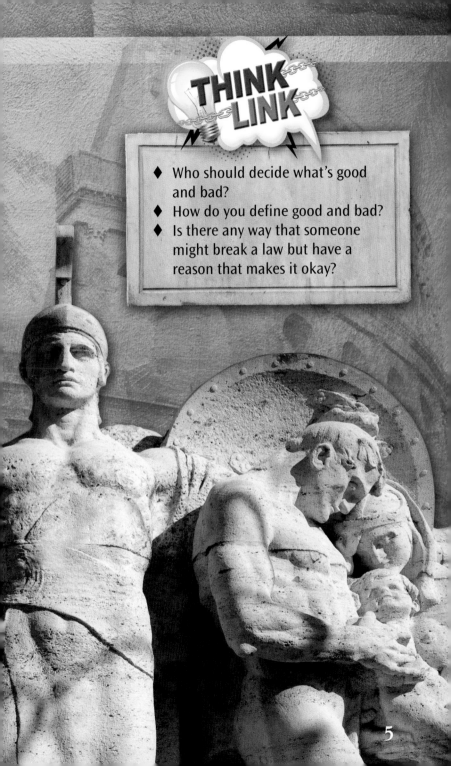

THINK LINK

◆ Who should decide what's good and bad?

◆ How do you define good and bad?

◆ Is there any way that someone might break a law but have a reason that makes it okay?

Ancient History

Ancient history marks the period from the beginning of time to the fall of the Western Roman Empire in AD 476. During that time, leadership **ebbed and flowed**. One group or person took power from another group or person until someone took it from them. And so it goes. The victors are remembered by history. And the deeds of some of the most rotten victors are remembered most of all.

Brutus
85 BC–42 BC

Antony
83 BC–30 BC

Caligula
AD 12–AD 41

Nero
AD 37–AD 68

Together, these leaders ruled over 9,000 miles of land!

Cleopatra
69 BC–30 BC

Locusta
AD 1?–AD 69

Cao Cao
AD 155–AD 220

Attila the Hun
AD 406–AD 453

THE ANCIENT WORLD

Throughout human history, the shape of continents and waterways has stayed much the same. But people in one area of the world knew little about people elsewhere—or even that "elsewhere" existed. For most people, the world only extended as far as they could walk. Take a look at how maps changed as people's understanding of the world grew.

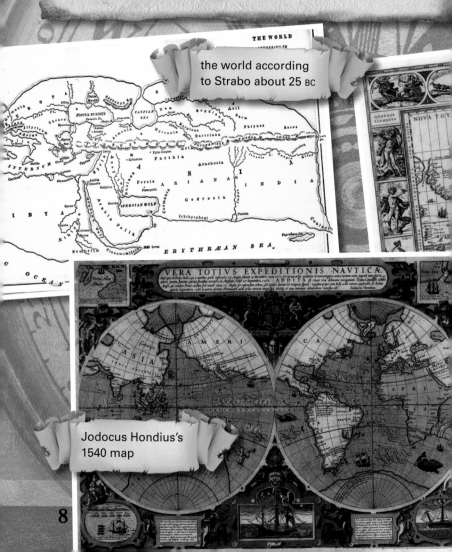

the world according to Strabo about 25 BC

Jodocus Hondius's 1540 map

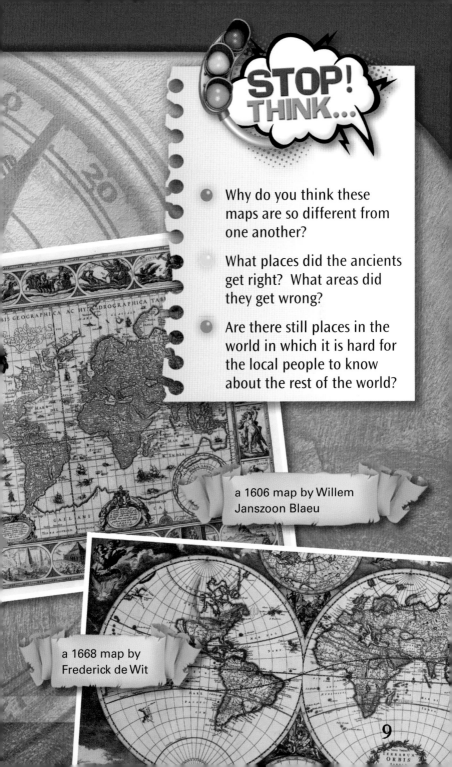

STOP! THINK...

- Why do you think these maps are so different from one another?

- What places did the ancients get right? What areas did they get wrong?

- Are there still places in the world in which it is hard for the local people to know about the rest of the world?

a 1606 map by Willem Janszoon Blaeu

a 1668 map by Frederick de Wit

How Do We Know?

How can we be sure the ancient stories are true? There weren't newspapers then. There weren't cameras to shoot events in real time. But people remembered stories that mattered, and they told those stories to others. Then, the others told the stories, too. Sometimes, they put the stories into songs. And as soon as they could, they wrote them down.

Whoops!

Sometimes even modern newspapers get the facts wrong. Here are a few REALLY big mistakes.

"Passengers Safely Moved and Steamer Titanic Taken in Tow"
April 15, 1912, Christian Science Monitor

"Dewey Defeats Truman"
November 3, 1948, Chicago Tribune

"Air Battle Rages Over Los Angeles"
February 25, 1942, Los Angeles Examiner

But perhaps, just like in the game of telephone, stories were told from one person to another until the story became very different from the way it was. Can we be sure that the ancient stories really happened the way we heard them? Maybe not. But historians look for evidence, and they are pretty sure that these stories happened. And if nothing else, they make good stories!

The famous storyteller Homer sings to a crowd.

HAMMURABI'S CODE

Bad guys and gals have existed longer than laws have. The Babylonian ruler Hammurabi wrote some of the earliest laws in 1772 BC . Called the Code of Hammurabi, it consisted of 282 laws and punishments. The punishments differed depending on the status of the person. The harshest punishments were for slaves, the lowest class of people at the time.

Stole from the market?

Lose an ear.

Hit your parents?

Say goodbye to your hands. They are about to be chopped off.

Accused someone of a crime they didn't commit?

Death is the penalty.

Stole from a burning house?

You shall be burned alive.

Drank too much alcohol?

It's time to drown.

Code of Hammurabi carved in stone

Brutus
With Friends Like These...

One of history's bad guys may have been a good guy caught up in a bad plan—all with people who ultimately turned on him, too. Marcus Junius Brutus was born within the vast and powerful Roman Empire. His father was a political rebel who was killed. Brutus was adopted by his uncle. He began his own political career at this time.

Marcus Junius Brutus

When Brutus was adopted, he changed his name to Quintus Caepio Brutus. But later, he went back to his birth name.

The full saying is, "With friends like these, who needs enemies?" What do you think it means?

Powerful Partners

Brutus worked for Cato, the governor of Cyprus. Cato was a strong man who was known for his **integrity**, and Brutus admired him. Brutus became known for being loyal and trustworthy, too.

As Julius Caesar, the leader of the empire, grew more powerful, he accepted Brutus among his most trusted friends. As leader, Caesar had great power. When the government declared Caesar **dictator** for life, several officials were troubled. They figured that Caesar would want to get rid of them. So they decided to get rid of Caesar first.

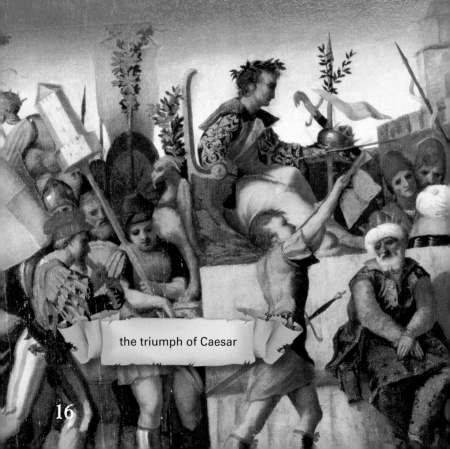

the triumph of Caesar

Beware the Ides of March

March 15 is known as the Ides of March. When people say, "Beware the Ides of March," they mean to be wary of false friends. The line comes from William Shakespeare's play, *Julius Caesar*, in which a fortune teller warns Caesar about the day he will be killed.

Julius Caesar

Betrayal

Brutus, fearful of Caesar's growing power, sided with the **traitors**. He helped to plan the **assassination**. On March 15, Caesar was stabbed 23 times by the attackers, including Brutus. The attack was so fierce the attackers even stabbed themselves in the frenzy.

The attackers were not charged with a crime. But this made the public angry. Brutus went into hiding for two years. When he and the others were finally charged with murder, Brutus and his army fought back. They were defeated. Knowing he would be captured, Brutus took his own life.

Brutus and other Roman senators assassinate Caesar.

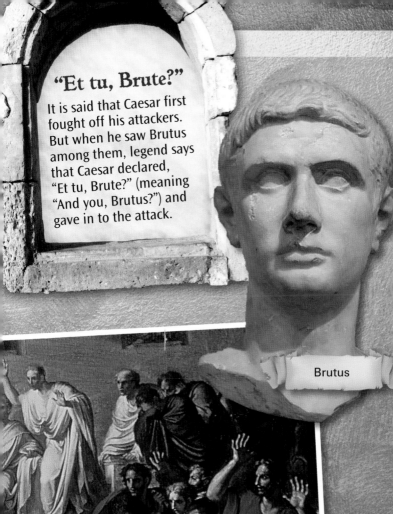

"Et tu, Brute?"

It is said that Caesar first fought off his attackers. But when he saw Brutus among them, legend says that Caesar declared, "Et tu, Brute?" (meaning "And you, Brutus?") and gave in to the attack.

Brutus

Worth a Thousand Words

There aren't any photographs from ancient times. So we don't know exactly how horrible these bad guys and gals appeared. Sculptures and paintings from artists that knew them or artists that heard stories about them help us imagine what these people looked like.

Antony and Cleopatra
Power Hungry

Mark Antony was born to a **ne'er-do-well** father. As a young man, he was a gambler and got into trouble. He went to Athens to escape his problems. There, he became an important soldier and a good friend to Caesar.

> Both Antony's father and grandfather were named Mark Antony.

actor Herbert Beerbohm as Mark Antony in 1907

engraving from a 19th century edition of Shakespeare's *Antony and Cleopatra*

Antony and Cleopatra.
Act 4. Sc. 10.

Mark Antony was born
January 14, 83 BC, and died
August 1, 30 BC

21

A Helping Hand

Antony helped Caesar free Italy of its enemies. His military victories were important, but he kept some of his old bad behaviors. When Caesar was killed, things looked bad for Antony. But he rose to power with the help of Octavian, Caesar's nephew and true successor.

Antony married Octavian's sister. But he later betrayed her with Cleopatra. Cleopatra was the last **pharaoh** of Egypt. She ruled with her father, then with her two brothers, and also with her son.

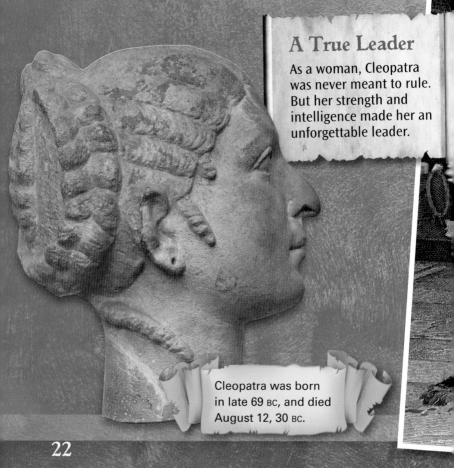

A True Leader

As a woman, Cleopatra was never meant to rule. But her strength and intelligence made her an unforgettable leader.

Cleopatra was born in late 69 BC, and died August 12, 30 BC.

It's All Greek

Cleopatra was really Greek. She was a member of the Ptolemaic Dynasty, a Greek family that once ruled Egypt. The family spoke only Greek—although Cleopatra spoke Greek and Egyptian—so Greek was used on official court documents.

Falling Stars

Egypt was troubled. Its cities were falling to Rome. Cleopatra did whatever she could do to protect her country. First, she had a relationship with Caesar to strengthen her power. They had a son, whom she trained to rule by her side. When Caesar was killed, she began a relationship with Antony. He was a rising star. Antony divorced his wife. He and Cleopatra had three children. They wanted to rule together and nearly did. But Octavian declared war on Antony. Antony killed himself when things became hopeless. Cleopatra did the same, with a bite from a poisonous **asp**.

Mark Antony, Cleopatra, and Julius Ceasar

For Love or Power?

Some say Cleopatra never truly loved these men. They think she only used them to gain power. Others say she was doing what was best for her country. Or perhaps she truly loved Caesar and Antony. The truth may be lost to history.

a poisonous asp

25

Caligula
Good Guy Gone Bad

At just 25 years of age, Caligula—the golden boy of the Roman Empire—became its **emperor**. He was the son of a well-loved general. Caligula was the nickname given to him by his father's troops. The name means "little soldier's boot."

When Caligula was just seven years old, his father died. Later, Caligula's grandfather, the emperor, died. That left Caligula as the only surviving male in his family. And that meant that when the emperor died, Caligula **succeeded** him.

History remembers Caligula as a good leader for the first two years of his four-year **reign**. He was noble and just. He helped people in tough times and made government records public. But then, the need for power took over. Caligula used power for his own pleasure. He had **lavish** homes built for himself. He became known for excess and for cruelty. He even had some of his family members **exiled** or killed. It is said that he forced one man to kill himself.

Emperor Tiberius

Caligula was born on August 31, AD 12, and was assassinated on January 24, AD 41.

Caligula's uncle Claudius

Many historians and writers of the time called Caligula insane.

Caligula and his aides receive foreign guests.

Unstoppable

Caligula used public money for many construction projects. Some helped the people, such as the **aqueducts**. But many were for himself. His **ego** grew. He called himself a god and made his subjects worship him. His spending created a financial crisis.

The **senate** wanted to get rid of Caligula and restore the **republic**. They had Caligula killed. On January 24, AD 41, at least 30 attackers stabbed Caligula to death. They killed some of his family, too. But his Uncle Claudius escaped and became emperor. The empire continued after all.

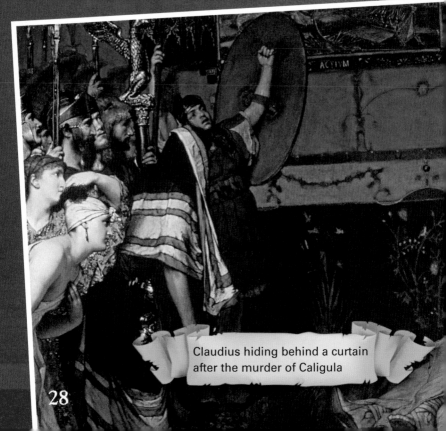

Claudius hiding behind a curtain after the murder of Caligula

Caligula's hair was thin and bald on top, though his body was very hairy. That made him look like a goat, but one could be put to death for mentioning a goat in his presence.

Cruel Leader

It is said that during a public event in which criminals were to be tried and thrown to wild animals to be killed, no criminals were available. So, Caligula picked a random section of the audience and had them thrown to the animals instead—just for fun.

29

GLADIATORS

Ancient leaders weren't the only people with shaky **ethics**. Ordinary people also enjoyed power and cruel forms of entertainment. Gladiators were slaves and criminals who were given another chance at freedom. But it came at a high cost. They were trained to fight in ancient Roman sporting competitions. Only the strongest survived.

Thumbs down meant the crowd wanted the gladiator to die.

A trumpet sounded to announce the fighting would begin.

Gladiators fought each other, as well as wild animals such as lions, crocodiles, and panthers.

The games were outlawed in AD 325.

The crowd could wave their handkerchiefs to show they wanted to make the fight easier for the gladiator.

The winner threw down his helmet so the spectators could see his face.

31

Nero
Fear and Fire

Nero was born into a royal family. His great-uncle Claudius adopted him so he could become emperor of Rome one day. When Claudius died, that's what happened. Nero ruled for 14 years. But when his reign ended, so did the reign of his family.

Just like Caligula, Nero did many things for the good of the people. Nero improved the culture of Rome. He held sporting games. He built theaters. He also improved trade. But at the same time, Nero spent a lot of Rome's money on himself. He built estates and lived in the best way possible. A terrible fire swept through Rome. It destroyed most of the city, including many fancy homes on a hill. They say, "Nero **fiddled** while Rome burned." Many people think Nero set the fire. Afterward, he used the land on the hill to build his dream estate.

Nero's estate was known as Domus Aurea, or Golden House.

Nero watches from a safe distance as Rome burns.

Nero was born on December 15, AD 37, and died on June 9, AD 68, at the age of 30. Nero became emperor in AD 54.

33

A High Cost

To pay for everything, Nero taxed heavily. People rebelled. Leaders wanted to take power from Nero. In an organized plan, Nero's guards and friends left him and he was named a public enemy. Nero tried to kill himself. Unable to do it, he looked for help. Finally, he found a servant to kill him and others to dig his grave. Nero was stabbed and bled to death.

It is unclear whether Nero felt any remorse for his terrible actions.

Persecutor

The early days of the Christian faith were marked with **persecution**. Nero was one of the first persecutors. It is said that he captured Christians and lit them on fire to light his grounds, the same way someone might light a tiki lamp.

Oh, Mama!

How bad is bad? Nero executed his own mother. He probably also poisoned his stepbrother. Interestingly, his mother was probably behind the death of Nero's uncle—in order to secure power for her son.

Agrippina the Younger, Nero's mother

Lions and tigers are released on Christians.

Locusta
Poison Ivy

Locusta was very good at her work. What did she do? She poisoned people. Locusta knew a lot about plants. She knew what could heal and what could harm. She especially knew what could kill.

Locusta poisoning a slave

Locusta was born sometime in the first century and died in January of AD 69.

Hemlock and belladonna were two of the most commonly used poisonous plants in Locusta's time.

Food Tasters

At the time, it was common for people in power to have servants who were food tasters. The food tasters would try the food and wine before the ruler did. If the food taster got sick or died, the ruler wouldn't eat or drink. Clearly, that plan didn't work well for everyone!

Death Becomes Her

When Agrippina wanted to kill her husband, Claudius, so that her son Nero could be emperor, she turned to Locusta. Locusta used poisonous mushrooms. They became Claudius's last meal. Locusta was sentenced to death. But Nero stepped in. Having Locusta on his side could be useful. If he got rid of his step-brother (and cousin) Britannicus, then Nero could rule. And that was the end of Britannicus.

Nero paid Locusta very well. She lived the high life. Others used her services, too. People knew what she did, and Locusta was often arrested. Yet she was always cleared. But the end of Nero's reign meant the end of Locusta. A few months after he killed himself, she was sentenced to death—and that time, there was no one to save her.

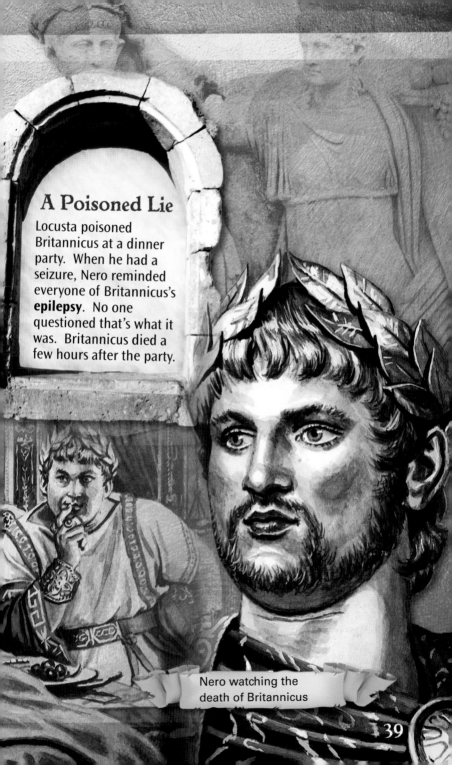

A Poisoned Lie

Locusta poisoned Britannicus at a dinner party. When he had a seizure, Nero reminded everyone of Britannicus's **epilepsy**. No one questioned that's what it was. Britannicus died a few hours after the party.

Nero watching the death of Britannicus

ALL IN THE FAMILY

In ancient times, power seemed to run in the family. Leaders were often related to each other. And even those who weren't related often had bad blood between them.

Gaius Octavius ♥ Atia
d. 59 BC (niece of
Julius Caesar)
d. 43 BC

Scribonia ♥ Augustus ♥ Livia ♥ Tiberius
?–? 63 BC–AD 14 58 BC–AD 29 Claudius Nero
d. 58 BC

Marcus Agrippa ♥ Julia Tiberius ♥ Vipsania
c. 63–12 BC (Elder) 42 BC–AD 37 ?–?
39 BC–AD 14

Gaius Lucius Agrippa Agrippina ♥ Germanicus
20 BC–AD 4 17 BC–AD 2 12 BC–AD 14 (Elder) 15 BC–AD 19
c. 14 BC–AD 33

Nero (Elder) Drusus Caligula
AD 6–30 AD 7–33 AD 12–41

Nero was the last emperor of the Julio-Claudian Dynasty.

40

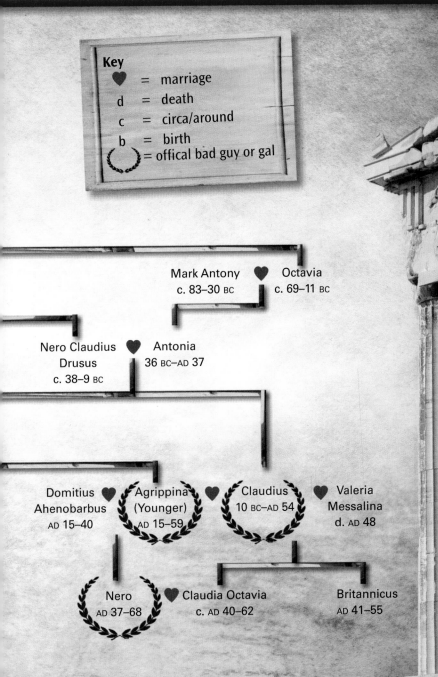

Key

♥ = marriage

d = death

c = circa/around

b = birth

🏵 = offical bad guy or gal

Mark Antony
c. 83–30 BC ♥ Octavia
c. 69–11 BC

Nero Claudius
Drusus
c. 38–9 BC ♥ Antonia
36 BC–AD 37

Domitius
Ahenobarbus
AD 15–40 ♥ Agrippina
(Younger)
AD 15–59 ♥ Claudius
10 BC–AD 54 ♥ Valeria
Messalina
d. AD 48

Nero
AD 37–68 ♥ Claudia Octavia
c. AD 40–62

Britannicus
AD 41–55

Cao Cao

Speak of the Devil

"Speak of the devil." This saying is said when someone arrives just as others are talking about him or her. In China, there is a similar saying: "Speak of Cao Cao (TSOW TSOW), and Cao Cao will be there." It means, if you talk about the devil, the devil will be there.

Cao Cao was one of the most powerful generals in Chinese history. He was a **warlord** and created his own state across northern China.

Cao Cao was born in AD 155 in Luoyang, China, and died on March 15, 220

Words of Wisdom

During Cao Cao's youth, a wise man of the time is said to have predicted that Cao Cao would be a capable minister in peaceful times and an unscrupulous hero in chaotic times.

Cao Cao had 25 sons! He probably had a couple dozen daughters, too. But they weren't considered important enough to be officially counted.

Military Minded

There are different stories of Cao Cao's rule. He has been remembered as cruel and without mercy. But historians now think that he was really a great military leader. And, perhaps, he was kind to those he ruled. Either way, Cao Cao's power came through victory in war. He fought his way to the top.

Cao Cao was highly skilled in martial arts.

Save the Wheat

Cao Cao and his soldiers once came upon a wheat field. Cao Cao declared that any soldier who trampled the wheat would be beheaded. But then, Cao Cao's own horse startled and trampled the wheat. Cao Cao wasn't about to behead himself, so he changed the sentence to chopping off one's hair—and then cut his own.

After his death, Cao Cao was named Emperor Wu of Wei.

Cao Cao's tomb in central China

Hungry for More

Cao Cao was the son of the emperor's favorite servant. As a teen, he often broke rules and used his wits to get ahead. At 20 years old, he got his first government job. He maintained strict rules. Cao Cao had lawbreakers **flogged** outside his offices.

Cao Cao began a series of war efforts and grew in power. He was once thought to control a million soldiers. Chinese legends described him as having evil magical powers. He was also a good planner. He built farms to feed the people. Cao Cao left many writings when he died, including great poetry and journals. It seems that he was also a lover of the arts.

Cao Cao's 1,700-year-old tomb was discovered in late 2008.

In Appreciation of the Arts

During his life, Cao Cao had a large terrace built on which musicians and dancers could perform. He then ordered that his tomb be built in view of the terrace, so that his children could see his tomb and so that his ghost could watch the performers from his tomb.

a mask of Cao Cao used in a Chinese opera

Caesar and Cao Cao both died on the Ides of March.

Attila the Hun
The Scourge of God

When people think of bad guys from long ago, they get a mental picture. They see a dirty, muscled man in a pointed fur hat. He probably has a shaggy moustache and a wild look in his eyes. They see Attila the Hun, one of the most feared leaders of ancient times.

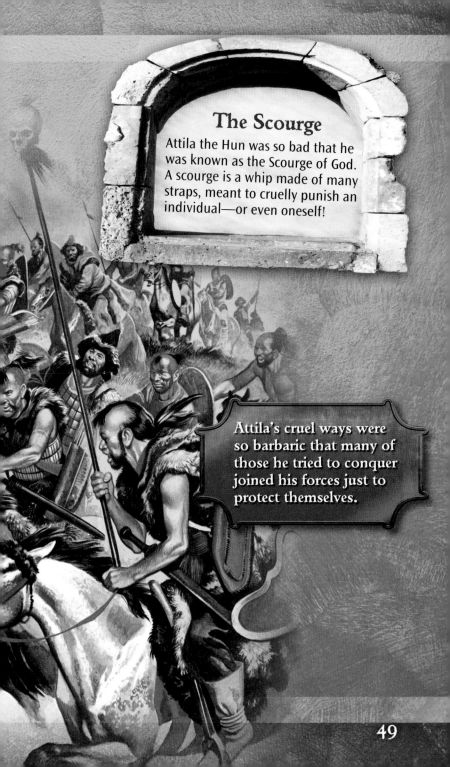

The Scourge

Attila the Hun was so bad that he was known as the Scourge of God. A scourge is a whip made of many straps, meant to cruelly punish an individual—or even oneself!

Attila's cruel ways were so barbaric that many of those he tried to conquer joined his forces just to protect themselves.

A Fearsome Reach

Attila became the ruler of the Huns in AD 434. He led by using fear and cruelty for about 20 years. The Huns were **nomads**. They **rampaged** Europe for about 300 years, striking terror in all.

When Attila came into power, he turned his sights on Europe. In 441, he swept through Eastern Europe. He then looked to Western Europe. He conquered many countries, but he could not take Rome.

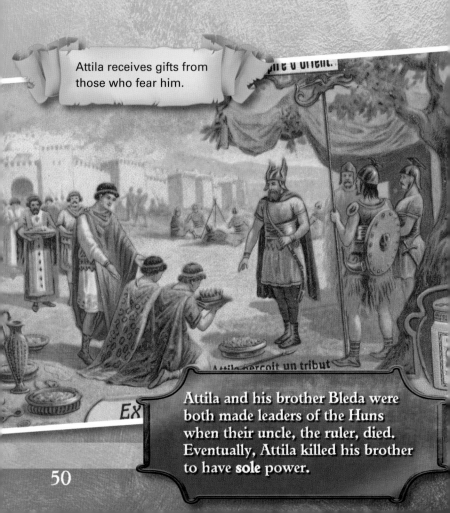

Attila receives gifts from those who fear him.

Attila and his brother Bleda were both made leaders of the Huns when their uncle, the ruler, died. Eventually, Attila killed his brother to have **sole** power.

Great Lengths

The Huns may have **originated** in Mongolia, near China. The Chinese began building at least part of the Great Wall to defend themselves against the Huns.

Ancient artists showed Attila's animal nature by adding a goat-like beard and devil horns to his portraits.

Attila's capital

At its peak, the Hun empire covered much of present day Europe and Asia.

51

A Bloody End

The Huns destroyed every place they fought. Under Attila, they were cruel and fierce and showed little mercy. Attila was hugely successful in battle. But he died a terrible death anyway. On his wedding night, he got an awful nosebleed that gushed blood. He bled to death, drowning in his own blood. Some believe he may have been poisoned.

Attila's sons fought for leadership after his death. But other tribes invaded, and the Hun's fierce rule soon came to an end.

Attila was born about AD 406 and died in 453.

To terrorize their foes, Attila and his army tied the severed heads of their victims to their saddles.

The Simple Stirrup

What gave the Huns a competitive edge over others? They used stirrups when riding their horses. The stirrups' metal frame supported their feet. This increased their leverage and balance when using weapons on horseback.

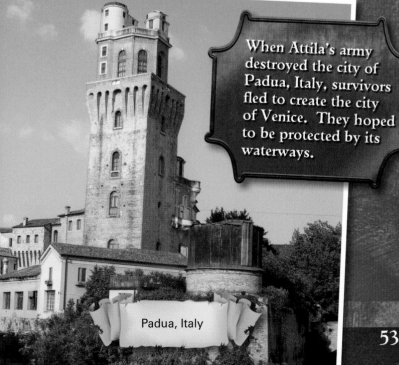

When Attila's army destroyed the city of Padua, Italy, survivors fled to create the city of Venice. They hoped to be protected by its waterways.

Padua, Italy

THE GREAT WALL OF CHINA

The Great Wall of China was built over many centuries. It was made to protect the people of China from invaders, including the Huns. It is a massive structure, made of a series of tall, sturdy walls and trenches, measuring about 5,500 miles long in all.

horse road

water spout

drainage ditch

shooting hole

watch hole

Bad or Good?

Who's to say whether the people in this book were really bad or good? Who's to say how the people of today will be remembered thousands of years from now? And in the end, is anyone ever really all bad or good?

How exactly will *you* be remembered?

Traitor: Ephialtes

Ephialtes was a nightmare to his countrymen the Spartans. He betrayed them to the Persians—all in the hope of a big reward. When the attacking Persians became stuck in a narrow passageway, Ephialtes secretly let them know a different way in to Sparta. The Spartans were surrounded—and destroyed! But the Spartans finally brought down the Persians, and Ephialtes lost out on his reward. He fled to protect himself, but he wasn't safe for long. He was eventually caught and killed. It seems he got his just reward in the end!

the Spartans fighting the Persians

Glossary

aqueducts—structures that carry water from a canal across a river or hollow area

asp—a poisonous snake

assassination—the murder of a government official

dictator—a ruler with absolute power

ebbed and flowed—the movement in and out of the tide; also a metaphor for the changing nature of things

ego—self-importance

emperor—the ruler of an empire, a country, or a region

epilepsy—a disorder that can cause people to suddenly become unconscious and have violent, uncontrolled movements of the body

ethics—rules of moral conduct

exiled—cast out of an area

fiddled—spent time in aimless activity

flogged—beaten with a whip

integrity—honesty and honor

lavish—expensive

ne'er-do-well—an idle, worthless person who never does anything good

nomads—wanderers who live in various places temporarily

originated—began, came from

persecution—continuous cruel or harmful treatment, often for religious or political beliefs

pharaoh—an ancient Egyptian ruler

plundering—stealing, especially openly and by force

rampaged—tore through with reckless and destructive behavior

reign—the time during which a ruler rules

republic—a government led by people elected by others to represent the wishes of the people

sabotaging—destroying or blocking progress performed by an enemy

senate—the supreme council of the ancient Roman republic and empire

sole—alone, shared by no one

succeeded—came after

traitors—people who betray another person or country

warlord—a military leader who governs an area by force

Index

Bibliography

Harvey, Bonnie. *Attila the Hun (Ancient World Leaders).*
Chelsea House Publications, 2003.

Take a glimpse at Attila's life in more detail. Learn about his childhood, study maps of the major milestones in his life, and learn about the battles that made him infamous.

Saunders, Nicholas, Dr. *The Life of Julius Caesar (Stories from History).* **Brighter Child, 2006.**

Take a fast-paced, factual look at Julius Caesar's rise to power in this graphic novel. Find out more about his successful rule and, ultimately, his assassination by one of his close friends. You know what they say—keep your friends close and your enemies closer.

Vennema, Peter and Diane Stanley. *Cleopatra (Time Traveling Twins).* **HarperCollins, 1997.**

This fun, well-crafted biography reveals what a lively and skillful ruler Cleopatra was. Learn about the love, wars, and strong desire for success that colored her life.

Whiting, Jim. *The Life and Times of Nero.*
Mitchell Lane Publishers, 2007.

The Roman emperor Nero was one of the most infamous people in ancient history. Discover more about his story in depth through this historical account.

More to Explore

Nero
http://www.pbs.org/empires/romans/special/emperor_game.html

Do you have what it takes to be an ancient Roman ruler? Here, you will have a chance to play as one of three Roman emperors, including Nero. Will you make some of the same decisions these famous rulers made?

Traitors and Villains of the Ancient World
http://www.funtrivia.com/quizzes/history/ancient_history.html

Choose *Roman History* to quiz yourself on some of the worst bad guys and gals from the ancient world.

Rome's Greatest Enemies Gallery
http://www.bbc.co.uk/history/ancient/romans/enemiesrome_gallery.shtml

Here, you will find six of Rome's most ruthless enemies. You'll find pictures, statistics, and the highlights of each of these bad guys' terrible deeds.

Agrippina the Younger
http://www.britannica.com/EBchecked/topic/9818/Julia-Agrippina

Learn more about Nero's mother and how she plotted against her husbands to secure her son's rule. Find out how powerful she really was and how she lost the power she had.

About the Author

Dona Herweck Rice grew up in Anaheim, California, and graduated from the University of Southern California with a degree in English and from the University of California at Berkeley with a credential for teaching. She has been a teacher in preschool through tenth grade, a researcher, a librarian, and a theater director, and is now an editor, a poet, a writer of teacher materials, and a writer of books for children. She is married with two sons and lives in Southern California, where she tries to be good.